A CHAMELEON BOOK

Jill's Dogs

Photographs by JILL FREEDMAN

POMEGRANATE ARTBOOKS
SAN FRANCISCO, CALIFORNIA

A CHAMELEON BOOK

Complete © 1993 Chameleon Books, Inc.
Text © 1993 Jill Freedman
Illustrations © 1993 Jill Freedman

Published by Pomegranate Artbooks
Box 6099, Rohnert Park, California 94927

Produced by Chameleon Books, Inc.
211 West 20th Street, New York, New York 10011

Creative director: Arnold Skolnick
Managing editor: Carl Sesar
Editorial assistants: Lynn Schumann, Nancy Crompton
Composition: Larry Lorber, Ultracomp
Printer: Oceanic Graphic Printing, Hong Kong

Library of Congress Catalog Card Number 93-84779

ISBN 1-56640-526-2

10 9 8 7 6 5 4 3 2 1

To Edie & Cornell Capa
Dr. Sven J. Kister
Kathy Moloney
Kent Karlsson
Michelle Andonian
and Jo Leggett
with thanks
and love.

Foreword

There is an essence to being a dog. It is an honor and it is a privilege, and in the appropriate setting, it can be a blessing. We have known about that for between 200 and 250 centuries.

There are people who are perceptive enough to realize the wonder of the canine state in a special way. Such a person, clearly, is photographer Jill Freedman. Jill explores the world of the dog with enormous sympathy, and in so doing, she captures the soul of dogginess as few other people have.

The great dog paintings of the nineteenth century fell into three categories. There were the sporting dogs, the purebred confirmation dogs, and the pet dogs whose owners wanted their companions immortalized.

Jill Freedman adds a fourth dimension. Jill, with a camera instead of a brush, creates an image because it is there, because it is wonderful and because she has been touched. We go along for the ride for we have been touched, too. It is in every way a joyride.

Roger A. Caras
PRESIDENT, THE AMERICAN SOCIETY FOR THE
PREVENTION OF CRUELTY TO ANIMALS

When I was little, I wanted a dog more than anything in the world, but my mother was allergic. I got a bike, skates, piano lessons, other things I wanted, and I got things I didn't want, like dolls, stupid dolls. I hated them. I wanted to be the kid, not the mother, and every kid needs a dog. Someone to play with and be nice to and he'll always love you and be your friend no matter what.　◇　When I finally grew up and got to New York, I passed a pet shop and a poodle pup caught my eye. When I brought him home, he followed me right into the kitchen, not scared of anything, my dog. I felt a sharp pang of love. New York, a room of my own, a dog, life was good. I named him Fang, for Jack London.　◇　We took care of each other. He kept off the lions, made me laugh, was always good for a cuddle. I sang him songs, fed him balanced meals, gave him vitamins. No chocolate, no single-malts, basic staples of my nutritional regimen. "This isn't good for dogs," I'd say, downing another dark truffle.　◇　Fang was the prettiest dog I ever saw. He was smart and eager, never mean; he didn't eat books, pee on beds, or threaten people. He was affable. You could pet him even when he wasn't in the mood, and when he was, he didn't moon about, sighing and staring at you like a tiresome lover. He liked other dogs, but he stood up to bullies, even when he was scared. You could hear his voice go up a little. A gentleman and, being a poodle, a natural clown, he had a great sense of humor and a big grin. I couldn't get over him.　◇　Fang loved being out. It's boring for smart dogs, shut up all day in an apartment. There's just so much napping and chewing a dog can do. So when he walked down that street, he didn't miss a thing. He saw and smelled and delighted in it all, nothing went unmarked. He saluted each tire, tree and hydrant, throwing his leg high and teetering like a wire-walker; and when he ran out of pee, he pissed air. He had great style, my dog.　◇　I had just started taking pictures then, and I became aware of things I had never noticed, details, though I had passed them countless times before. Fang was my teacher. He taught me how to see. We had wonderful adventures, and seeing through his eyes made everything new and strange and exciting. I was young and loved New York and making pictures, and I was lucky to have this great-hearted, loving being as my friend.　◇　I'm nuts about dogs. People often look like their dogs. I wish they'd act like them, too. Dogs are generous animals. You run into the odd crazy one, but dogs are so kind, so courteous. They are loving and loyal, and we could all use friends like that. They will tolerate things that bore them to death, just so they won't hurt your feelings. They're nice that way. ✧ I often think how wonderful it would be if we were more like dogs. Dogs are so happy when they see another dog. Think how friendly it would be if we were like that, happy to see other people. We'd see someone we like and run right up, take a sniff, say hello, instead of turning away, regretting it later. Better a dog than a chicken. ✧ Dogs never forget how to play. Old dogs have as much fun as puppies. They're up for everything. They have the curiosity of a child, and they never lose it. They are always high. Lucky dogs. ✧ Dogs are not snobs. No pedigree will stop one from eating out of the garbage, drinking out of the toilet, or lying down with fleas. They don't care if a dog is white, black, or yellow, to the manor or the hovel born. There are only two questions here: does this dog bite, and will he play? ✧ People think they're so much smarter than dogs. Right. How come we don't understand their language? They understand ours. Dogs don't work jobs they hate. They run, they sleep, they're thrilled when you get home. For that they get room, board, and love. ✧ Dogs don't have our hang-ups. You can always tell when they're happy or sad, they bark, they howl, they know what to do. When I got my first real job—one I badly wanted—Fang and I barked and rolled around together on the floor. What a good time. I've never told that before. ✧ Dogs are bum-rapped for the things humans do to them. Dogs don't care about mink coats or diamond collars. They don't sit around putting little bows in their ears. No dog will turn you down because you're broke. And if a dog is vicious, it is usually a human who made him that way. ✧ Dogs behave better than we do. They have better manners. They don't soil their nests. They're gentle with puppies. They don't dump their people when they want new ones. They enjoy life. They're there to do their job, which is to make us happy. No wonder we like them. If they could cook, we'd marry them. ✧ They're funny to watch. One day I saw two dogs, separated by a fence, stalking along, yelling and snarling like hellhounds. Suddenly there was no more fence, it just stopped. It was like two guys in a bar, "Hold me back, I'll murder him!" The shock on those two dogs' faces. They stopped dead and stared at each other, time suspended, then turned

around and started back along the fence again, barking and carrying on like before. ✧ I learned another thing from a dog I never forgot. I was walking down MacDougal Street and there was this funny-looking dog walking towards me. He was so silly-looking, I laughed. He looked at me with such a hurt expression, it made me feel bad. "I'm not laughing at you, I'm laughing with you," I told him, but we both knew better. I felt ashamed. I have never laughed at another dog since, at least not when he could see me. ✧ Sometimes I accost strange dogs on the street, petting and talking to them. I often don't even notice who they're with, unless it's another dog. This has been brought to my attention and I say the hell with it. ✧ I notice I'm not the only one greeting strange canines on the street. I watched a man chatting away to an embarrassed lady dog who was trying to catch a little sun in the park. I understand. You're walking along, probably feeling good, and here is this soft furry being, bursting with good vibes, and you just want to touch it. ✧ I AM crazy about dogs. I admire them enormously. Noble beasts, always saving people's lives, pulling them out of rivers, scaring off thugs, finding lost kids. They are our oldest friends. Dogs will die for us. Better yet, they will live with us, and it's much more fun with a dog around. I know why we like them, but why do they like us? ✧ Dogs are damn good company. You can take them walking or fishing, or just sitting in the moonlight, and they won't talk your ear off. Dogs know how to keep quiet. One of the nicest dogs I ever met was in Ireland, a gentle soul who sat beside me on a hillside one summer's day. Later I saw him escorting his lady cows home. ✧ They say that some men would sell their children before they'd sell their dog. I can see that. Dogs are cheaper, and they won't grow up and leave you. Unlike women, they're happy with only one man, and they need to be submissive. No one likes you more than your dog. He isn't after you to shave or make a living. You don't have to buy him gifts. Just throw him a bone, and he could care less that you lost your job or hate your life or have three heads. He thinks you're the greatest thing that ever walked, and he'll tell you so every time you come home, even if it was just down to the corner for a six-pack. ✧ Sometimes they're our only friend. There's no ugly to a dog. They allow us to take care of them, and they take care of us. They make us laugh. They're good for our health, our heart, our liver. Some work in nursing homes and hospitals. Dogs don't care about wrinkles; they don't judge or criticize, they make you feel loved and needed, no matter how young or old or screwed-up you are. Dogs are good for you. ✧ And they're fun. They don't sit around bitching about nothing to do. They are always up for adventure. Sometimes people jog with their dogs. I wish I were a dog, I'd chase joggers, the sweaty ones in their underwear. But city dogs have to be leashed, so they don't get much running in. It's like you only see fat lions in the zoo. Some dogs get to run in the park and I love watching them play. They know their parole is a short one and then it's back to stir, so they get in all the fun they can. It's nice watching innocence, even if it is a dog. No beach is complete without one. ✧ I have always loved and admired dogs for their dogginess, because they ARE dogs. I never saw them as little furry people. They are nothing like people, they are like dogs, a nicer species. I love watching them, playing with them, knowing them. I wish I were more like a dog, but I'm working on it. Sometimes people say my dog pictures look like they were taken by another dog. I love that. I was probably a dog in another life. Maybe that's why I chase fire engines.

—Jill Freedman

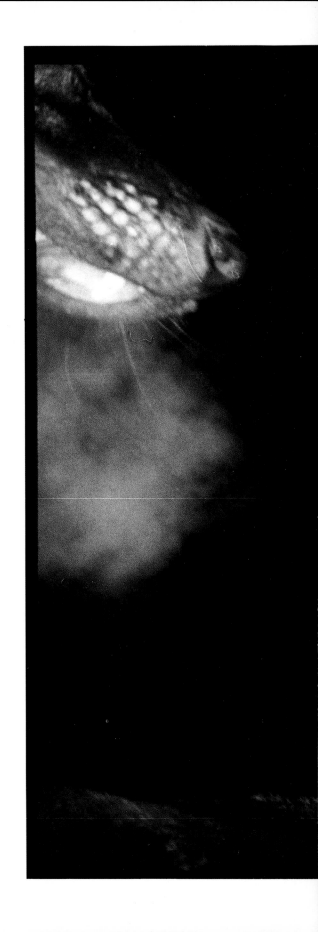

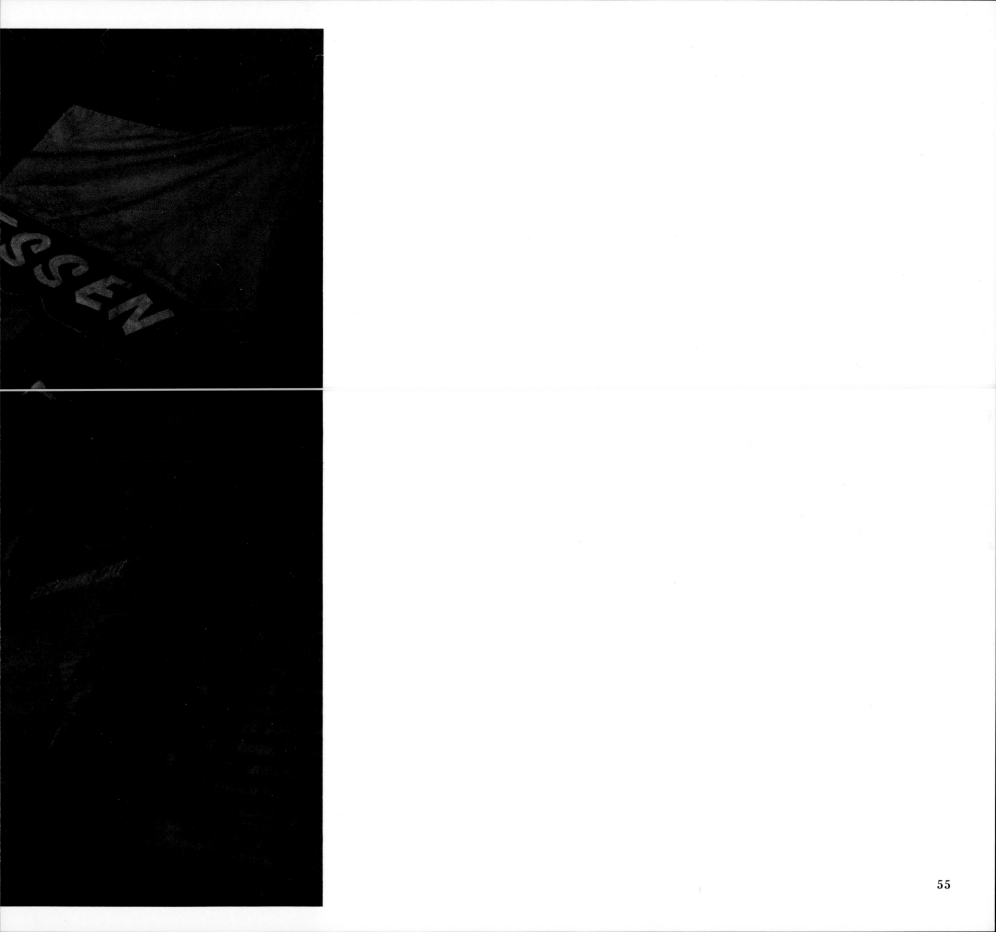

FANG and I, 1967